praise

"A vivid, unexpected gut-kick, rarely seen in poetry. Jessica Bell's voice is a terrifying mix of crying child, angry teen, and screaming adult heard inside the rock and roll tornado of abuse. Her use of music and unique form create a vibrating song of poems demanding to be heard. Readers will remember TVC 's haunting chords long after the last stanza is struck."
ALAINE DIBENEDETTO BENARD, POET AND ARTIST

"Through the poet's adept and generous use of clipped lines, staccatos, onomatopoeia, smells, and descriptions of icky body fluids, these poems tell the story of a mother and daughter hopelessly linked by love and hate. Jessica Bell doesn't let up. She is a genius at portraying the raw and dark parts of life through her use of words and where she places them on the page. This is an exciting and wonderful read."
MADELINE SHAPLES, CO-EDITOR OF THE GREAT AMERICAN POETRY SHOW, VOLUMES 1 AND 2

"A bold, unique voice, Jessica Bell's words leap into existence with the bravery of raw, vivid imagery and language aimed straight at the heart of the matter. Masterful, lyrical and haunting, *Twisted Velvet Chains* is a pulls no punches approach to tackling painful, delicate subject matter with a refined skill and subtle grace."
DEBBIE BERK, EDITOR OF THE STRAY BRANCH

"A collection of fractured memories viewed through the kaleidoscope of a tortured mother-child relationship. Even if the side effects of reading may be a bit of nausea and dizziness, you can't extract yourself from Bell's twisted poetic chains until you've read them all."
ANGIE LEDBETTER , CO-PUBLISHING EDITOR OF ROSE & THORN

about the author

Jessica Bell is an Australian award-winning author and poet, writing and publishing coach, and graphic designer who lives in Athens, Greece. In addition to her novels and poetry collections, and her best-selling *Writing in a Nutshell* series, she has published a variety of works online and in literary journals, including *Writer's Digest*.

Jessica is also the Co-Founder and Publisher of *Vine Leaves Press & Literary Journal*, a singer/songwriter/guitarist, a voice-over actor, and a freelance editor and writer for English Language Teaching publishers worldwide such as Macmillan Education and Education First.

Before she started writing she was just a young woman with a "useless" Bachelor of Arts degree and a waitressing job.

Visit Jessica's website: *jessicabellauthor.com*

Vine Leaves Press
Melbourne, Victoria, Australia

Second Edition
ISBN-13: 978-1-925417-42-5

First edition published independently in Australia, 2011

Cover design by Jessica Bell
Interior design by Amie McCracken

National Library of Australia Cataloguing-in-Publication entry (pbk)
Creator: Bell, Jessica Carmen author.
Title: Twisted velvet chains / Jessica Bell.
Edition: 2nd edition
ISBN: 9781925417425 (paperback)
Subjects: Manic-depressive illness--Poetry.
Drug addiction--Poetry.
Mothers--Poetry.
Dewey Number: A821.4

twisted velvet chains

jessica bell

Vine Leaves Press
Melbourne, Vic, Australia

For those who feel they don't quite belong.

contents

part III

part IV

bipolar tongues

Excuses abuse trust
she said
Mummy said
my mother said
and my mum said

They all said
Excuses
abuse trust

It was
the sanest thing
she *ever* said
because they all
said
it.

It came from her,
not *them*;
not the ones
that spoke in
bipolar tongues …

part 1

bird poop spun by rumpelstilzchen

You give me a stool to stand on
so we can wash dishes together.
Chatter—*Belinda said*—chatter
Daddy said—chatter—blah blah
blah—stutter—*What you think?*
Very first time you ask my
opinion, and I blank out. It turns
into a habit—this blanking; Blanco;
blacking out. Suds between fingers;
foam. Whoever said you couldn't
hold air? *Look, Mummy! You want
a cappuccino?* I offer her a tea cup
full of fluffy bubbles—the one with
blue birds flying round the rim, on
flecks of gold—bird poop spun by
Rumpelstilzchen. Tweet, tweet.
Squeak, squeak. *Eek! What's that?*
Mummy drops a saucer on the
kitchen floor. Daddy hung a rubber
tarantula by the window in a vine.
She thought it was real. Is he nuts?
I guess we all are around Mummy.

doctor, doctor, darling, sweetie, cuddle, cuddle everything

on bed—stuffed toys
—sick—*Doctor*
Doctor—feed them jelly
—just like on TV
injection—sewing needle
—masking tape
invention—consolations
—*Darling, Sweetie*
when they wince
—cuddle, cuddle
tell them; *here, here.*

You're just going to feel
a little discomfort, Dear.

Chop!

out
infected splinter
too afraid
to reveal it
cover it
with sleeve for weeks.

Shh …

better than home

Strawberry ice cream and dessert dirt clog nose
Putty filling useless organ—oxygen apertures
Masks fake smiles, eyebrows black—thick slugs

Move!

Dry weed tufts tickle ear—wisps of smell with sound
Bruised flesh round upper arm—Chinese lunch time burn
My excuse to save Mummy.

vibrations

Vibrations whistle—
Rattle. Hum.
Lamp shade buzz.
Same words sung.
Over. Over.
E-string strum—
Repeat. Repeat.
Ooh-ooh. Ah-ahs.

Four-track mixer
clicking, winding—
Guitar cable
Crackle. Crackle.
Amplifier
Wah-wah. *Wow.*
Daddy's thrill.
Mummy's pill.

Fake pregnancy
Stroke *mah* belly
Bicycle helmet
under nighty
Sing to it, teddy—
La, la. Ha, ha.
Mummy singing
in my womb.

the blob

Nude balls; marbles
glistening in the sun,
naive French kisses
on the sidewalk—
teens entranced, hooked
by tongues. Lawn
mower grumbles back
ground murmur.
Grape juice splashes
on her knees—below
elfin cherry blossom.
Nickel veiled behind
my ear. Did you hear
her laugh at my liquid
freckles?
Guffaw!
Interrupted
by gurgling phlegm; hits
pavement. I stare,
reminded of *The Blob*.
She calls as I run,
I trip.
My forehead cracks
against the red
tiled step.

scratch 'N' smell

Stickers—scratch 'n' smell.
Strawberry shortcake,
orange meringue,
moments of heaven
when I'm alone.

I block out your voice—sniff!
Hoarse—tired,
he lied again.
Please stay away
from the kitchen.

Stickers—scratch 'n' smell.
Peppermint chocolate,
cherry lane,
moments of heaven
when I'm alone.

I block out his moan—sniff!
Daddy—groan.
You stabbed him again.
Please stay away
from the bathroom.

Stickers—scratch 'n' smell.
Hubba Bubba,
lemon squash,
moments of heaven
when I'm alone.

I block out your scream—sniff!
Self-inflicted—fraught.
You cut yourself again.
Please stay away

from my bedroom.

Please stay away.
Please stay away
from my stickers.

carpet stinks of gaffer tape

Carpet stinks of gaffer tape
rough and raw
on my bare bottom
sticky like chewing gum

Thrown in the corner
to draw.
Bored.
I scratch
new bass guitar.
Stanley knife—
Um … accident.
I wanted to cut memory chords.

She whips me with
a cable.

Burns.

no TV for two months
no playing with the stupid snotty girl
across the road

It wasn't even hers.

I hate you.

Orange hair
Square jaw
Scared of you
Please don't

Please don't smash
my snow ball—

my pretty little snow ball
that sends me to sleep
when you're screaming at Daddy.

masks

Chocolate lipstick,
candy shoes.
Soft black pencils,
copper rouge.
Mummy, gimme
grey tulle—lace.
So I can hide
your wasted face.

gothic Neanderthal

I listen
Will it ever end?
Her gentle, velvety voice
mimicking childish sobs
amidst animal grunts

Head under pillow
Camping in Africa
on a space ship in Galactica;
an unseen witness to murder
in an abandoned
graffiti-coloured crime district

I cradle my teddy bear,
close to my chest,
covered head to toe
in my feathery nest.

I stroke it
whisper
You're not alone
I'm here. Shh, don't cry
Fingers in ears
so hard
it hurts

to avert
my ache—her cries—his
screeching—the insufferable thunderous thump
through thin floor

I climb out of bed,
creep down the hall,
peer through the crack
of the kitchen door.

Grey netting hangs
from naked papery breasts,
dark purple tulle
fastened round her waist
black smudges
smeared 'cross her face.
patterned like lace
wet stringy hair
sticks
to her brow
her neck
wet cotton
sweat
toxic breath
menstruation blood
the onion soup we ate for lunch—
I dry-wretch

It stops—silence
Her arms hover in the air.
Twisted grace, fit for a coffin

Did it die?

No.

Daddy strokes her like the cat
she nods—
whispers and purrs

Behind her come chants
Push, push! Push, push!
It begins again;
She screams—
note shrill against the beat

droning voices of back-up men

Gothic Neanderthal giving birth
Giving life
To song

blush

Pants down behind bus
Kneeling beside you
Warm yellow trickle
Damn!
Soiled shoe, smelly hand
Embarrassed now—adieu!
I bolt, giggle
leave you standing
drizzle, drizzle, drizzle …

rainbows rain girls

Rainbows rain girls,
she says.
She twirls
round in her long black skirt.
I sit cross-legged
on the carpet,
tracing coloured circles
on my pants
with my finger.
Rainbows rain girls,
she says.
Again.
I look up.
I say,
Does that mean I'm not a girl?
She stops spinning,
gazes out the window,
points to the front lawn.
I look too.
The sprinkler is squirting
a rainbow into the roses.
She frowns.
She says, nothing to
do with you, Sweetheart.
Just telling the ladies
a rainbow is raining.

phallus stiff

Step
       Slide
              Hip
                     Flick
chorus hiccups — phallus stiff
toxic breath — musician's static
mummy plays with plastic dick
                     Flick
              Hip
       Slide
Step

birthday

I get home
from school
and there
you all are
waiting
hushed
for me
to walk in
Surprise!

Ruined.
My birthday
ruined.
The first
day
you're sane
in almost
a month
and I'm forced
to spend
it eating
fairy bread—
drinking
lemonade,
sharing toys
with school kids
I don't even like.

I run away.
And snap your records.

flamenco fun

Cheek squashed
to your breast;
ear wet. Sweaty.
You grip too tight,
rock back and forth,
twist my head
toward the sun
searing freckles
on my face;
marks of misbehaviour.

I squirm
from your embrace
and run—
climb the fig tree
where I like to sing
for the grass,
and purple plums.

Legs wrapped
around thick branch
I pull myself
higher
trunk massaging
my vagina
I hold

my breath,
close my eyes
you scream
for me to come
down.

I won't.

You slap me
for making you
play. It's my fault
you ripped my dress.
It's my fault.
I forced you.

We were blowing bubbles.
It was fun.
We skipped up and down
the driveway.
You spun
round and round—
arms in air
smiling
in my fancy-dress
Flamenco frock.

Then you rode
my bicycle—
too small for you,
caught my skirt
in the spokes.
Destroyed.
My favourite dress destroyed.

For a moment,
I loved you.
For one moment.

infected

Blood drips
in my
hot milk—
sliced callous.

She
makes me
drink it.

Afraid I've
swallowed
mania, I vomit
in my sleep.

inverted beat

Moments before
you change,
movement becomes
scaled;
a robot
with
a plastic grin,
actions timed,
inverted
beat.
Bang!—plate
Clang!—spoon
Click!—tongue with attitude.
You send me
to my room to scrub
urine from the carpet
corner where I pissed
like a dog
last night
because
you accidentally
locked me in.

the fender

Hands clammy
on back,
I vomit
in the parking lot
from our dark red
V-Dub Beetle,
packed to the brim
—bassist in
boot—amplifier
in back seat—my first
migraine of many
to come.

Smile, said Mum,
as our Beetle
slowed to a stop.
License and registration
please, Ma'am.

She obliged,
smile more hesitant
than mine—you
got a fine, and sold
your Fender
to pay for it. Why
did I feel like that was
my fault, too?

school play

Dragon had drools and
spools muddy thread round my neck
rehearsal hanging

secret friends

I don't know how to pray,
but I've seen them do it
on TV; kneeling by a bed
in nightgowns, hands woven
like secret friends.

What do they say
when they embrace;
fingers side by side
like crayons in a box?

I've seen how children whisper
to fingers held close
to chins—Can fingers speak?
Well, of course, they can
when they're deaf,
but I can hear.

Perhaps that's why
I don't know how to pray.

all things that shine

You'd leave old shoes,
scrap tulle and ripped
sheets in my dress-up
basket during the night.

Every week I'd find
something new;
you'd try to mimic
pride—took me to
gigs. You'd even let
me wear sequins—
despite hating all
that shined. But I'd
cry if you'd refuse.

Before I understood
your moods, I wondered
whether someone took
shiny things from you too.

smells like soya milk

At five, forget pain. It only lasts as long as it lasts. Because she buys you ice cream. Afterwards. Drops you off at a babysitter's that smells like soya milk, tofu and marmite, rather than foundation, perfume and lipstick. Pain turns to a yearning for comfort—throbbing—emptiness trying to be born through tears—but you mute its exit with a pillow—a stranger's pillow, not even yours. The only thing you can do in this weird house to avoid inconveniencing them—mummy taught you manners. But when you realize you can't even feel sad in the comfort of your own home, you feel even sadder—emptiness finally birthed—and so are the never-ending nights you fall asleep with teeth clenched.

bent ballerina

Crooked cherry wilt
Ed—the bitch without reason
music box upturned

part II

frayed

Each coral strand of fringed lamp shade suffers
every time you mute the TV.

Paranoia lures you to the peep hole
and I watch you tw- tw- tw- twitch.

With each twitch, I pull a thread of fringe till
it unravels, the way each twitch

unravels me.

IN your jacket pocket

Visitors rattle you into panic. You knew it would happen when you looked in the empty cookie jar. Hands trembling—you fill it with water, muttering: Fucking hell. Fucking bullshit! Your red-hennaed hair blinks in sunshine; intuitively misjudged, innate, crunchy with gel; smells like wet autumn leaves and mud. You spit in your jacket pocket, so you don't lose your keys.

make me a star

I want to sing
on *Young Talent Time*.

I want to learn
River.

I want you
to teach me.

Make me
a star.

You train me.
I practice.

You say
I'm awful.

Are you trying
to protect me?

Or saving yourself
from being upstaged?

MORNINGS

Dried coal mascara
crumples from your temple.

I poke it to wake you.
Nostrils flare—phlegm quivers
in your throat when you try to speak.

So you point to the plastic bottle of courage;
finger shaking—nail bruised—knuckle swollen.

crossed wires

nothing	you	sing
can	break	this
curse	because	live
independent	music	and
guitar	tunes	fuse
thrashing	death	metal

cracked concrete or hungry fly?

Every day I wait
for   an   apricot
to ripen — to d
                r
                o
                p

            to   the   ground;
            land on cracked
            concrete / steps
            — ---- — ---- — -
            to rot or be eaten
            by   fruit flies. I
            know ... you'll d
                    r
                    o
                    p

                But when? What state
                will you be in? Ripe or
                rotten? What about me?

                        Will I crack or fly?

tears like ethanediol: Part I

I was half awake when she opened my door. From a half-squinted eye, I saw her dark silhouette—her breath a shadow on the floor. Framed in sunlight—a wan femme fatale lost in absence—bound in smoky decor. With red hennaed hair, waving like a flag, she lifted her fag to her mouth. In slow motion she parted her deep bronze lips, face enamored with smoke, cigarette pinched between forefinger and thumb like a bloke. I watched, clutching sheet to chin—clouds floating above my bed—lethargy looming like lead. I only closed my eyes for a moment when I felt the pain in my head. Like freedom. Mind frozen. Numb. She pulled my hair, I dropped to the floor, flung my arm against her shin, crawled along the carpet, and out my bedroom door. I locked her in.

tears like ethanediol: part II

Hysterical scream.
Smashing glass,
booming sheets,
words inexplicably abashed.
Silence traced my feet—
cold air through teeth.

Tap, tap.
Scratch, scratch.
Knocking wood?
A desperate groan.
Breath held.
Will I ever be
left alone?

Crash.

tears like ethanediol: part III

Fingers trembling I pushed open the door. Perhaps she's dead on the floor? No. In her hand, a mirror, a shattered edge, a reflection of cherry lace, blood smeared across her face, through her hair—

Negated grace.

She stood still, a possessed china doll, dried mascara-tinted tears like ethanediol. My mother, a breathing shell of hate, reached for me, her daughter—bait. Has she come to claim me too? Like she—

Did my father?

I closed my eyes tight, but she only cupped my head in her hands. Her pulse throbbed through my temples, fingers wet, cold—kind, a silent plead to love her, a violent plead to pluck her from disgust—

From darkness.

She lifted my lids. Dug her jagged nails into my skin. I whispered, *Empty*. She'd engraved it in the wooden frame of my bed. I began to cry. My tears stung. *Now you're like me*, she said. *You may live—*

*but within …
you'll feel dead.*

the locket

I got
a locket from
my Grandma. You
took it to keep it
safe. Gone now
forever.

brick grit

head on
brick grit
stuck in skin
ruby jewels
sand paper
tools
dissolving stitch
brush off
dry blood
red crumbs
in eyelash
paper cut sting
she still sings
please no more
poison stash

drunk to be different

Drunk on sex—kissing
cross-dressed boy in park with cask
wine in hand—escape.

Nailed

In Woodwork when
I nailed my thumb
to a handmade spoon
I thought of you.

I thought you'd enjoy
watching me scream—
watching the blood
gush—stain my brown
leather school shoes—
the ones I punctured
with bass clefs in Textiles.

I imagine you trying
to push my blood
in the holes.

black hole

Your beauty spot moves like your eyes flit at lit wicks.
Though you say it's a mystery mole, I don't think it is

—I think it's a black hole;

A cage of demons: women, men, children, red poppies.
Some days it's darker than others; depends on the light

—like your dark tart soul.

I'm afraid to touch it in case it bites. Where might I go?
In your mind? Where everybody is repeatedly bleating

—vulnerabilities leaking?

The voices hide in your red lips—your brow and pores.
Tame them; all those tongues who know not how I feel

—if I dare kiss the beauty

sp●t.

by tongues

My friends adored you.
When you'd pick me up
from school they'd stare
at your eyebrows—logos
of gothism—fake lesbianism.
You were a like a big sister;
rock 'n' roll baby!—the woman
they all wanted to be.

You'd invite them over
for afternoon tea.
You'd coax them into talking
about sex, masturbation,
homosexuals; you'd express
insight—*laissez-faire*
toward the boy who
tried on my school dress.

You'd trick them into
betraying my secrets—the girl
I pashed behind the shelter
shed; the one with epilepsy
who liked to lie and got
pregnant from my tongue.
My friends never knew
what happened after they left.

deformed

The strength of her grip
sears fingerprints
into my palm.
I'm silenced
as her claws embed
into my lifeline,
piercing what's been
patented as my stream
of consciousness
since I tore through
my mother's skin
like alien spores.
Have I been growing
like fungus;
spreading myself
as far as I can stretch—
for this day? For the day
I realize she,
who put me on this
earth, has the power
to extinguish me too,
by severing the link—
deforming my instrument.

NINE

more voddie
bessie, please
help me flee
from high
vi-si-t*or*
back yard
you me
don't make
me beg
hold hair
from face
while spew
over swing set
bed now?
man gone?
great!
must sleep
must be
pristine
Christmas play
to-*mah*-row
can't b*ah-rea*the
through mouth
not nat-ur-*ahl*
nose blocked
don't tell
your dad
i swallowed
n*igh*nnnnne …

failing frankenstein

Fire foreshadows failure. Have faith you say? You find me fickle? In this field of vision faith is fundamentally favourable. Fearlessness is frightful. I'm failing Frankenstein! I fret. I flout. I file my nails. Filling in time with futility. *Fuck you!* Is that feasible? Or simply fussy foolishness? Yes. Perhaps it is. Fondling the frail hope of trust, I watch it float fervently in front of me like a firefly. I flinch. It flirts. I flick it away. A fading fairyland. That's what this is. I'll find my ferocious flair one day. I will. I promise. I'll serve you with finesse. With a therapeutic fix on fervour. Fascinating, isn't it? Life? Fearlessness? Hope, love and all that inanity? *Fuck you?* Yes. Okay. I can accept that. *Fuck you, too.*

roll over

Tailor made lies
suit you like the rock
T-shirts you wear.

When are you
going to stop
being a pussy?

You say you're
a man.

Well I say you're
a fucking anemone
in a fish bowl the size
of my thumb nail.

Go on.
Roll over.
Pull your pants down.
Don't look at me like that.

Pout, pout.

Let her slap you
like she does in your dreams.

Yes. It's real.
Take it.
Guilt free.

No. It's not a joke.

You asked for it.

marionette

Braces latch onto china hems, holding me up;
subconscious—following bent cobbled trails,

pebbles sharp—guiding pincers scratch soles
of feet; broom handles dent sand. I wash light

out of secrets and doll moulds and cup-cakes.
Evil-eyes flush moods into minds, into shapes

of pain and tri-angles. I will not let you move
me—not anymore. For I'll become the puppet

… master when you're gone.

too good for me?

chic metal face
probe protection panels
venom purrs triumph

drowning in liquid dirt

Dig down deeper. Weaken your dreams. Watch debonair ducks wade round your feet; swans dying to escape distorted life. Deft yet deficient; trading dust for a dime. Dabble in the pond—dress thoughts with drizzling mud. Don't fade, sink or despond. Drive passion from the ground—distant from demons burning in defence. Will you abscond drowning in dirty water, or watery dirt? You didn't ordinarily respond. I'm the devil—you must disappear. Can't discharge the dead; surrender bloodshed. Liberate you from dread? My dear, you have one last chance. Desert me now, keep looking ahead.

electric chair

dreaming of
belligerent lecture
strapped to electric chair
not afraid to die, but afraid
to listen.   Must recite lyrics
over and over; block out the
voice; louder and louder our
screams unite when volume
loses power
So we

stop.

Stare.

Prepare for a hanging ins
t
e
a
d

up front

Lubricated jagged voice samples and chattering crowd hush like ebbing rain against her desperate distorted whining wail. Balance the deep groan—with bass—as it vibrates through the stage, through your legs, body, arms, tightening your throat—Can you sing with a clenched craw? Resist belligerent gothic toe-stepping lead guitarist—his hash-slash-beer-breath. Hold vibrato during drummer's rigorous off-beat toms; the asynchronous delayed electric grit as it unites with rhythm. But never upstage her. Ever. I like to see her at the front.

excreting insanity

Pain seeps through the crack
Below false wall
Swimming in sun—singing in dust
My bare feet in a spotlight
Varnish glitters on my toes
Floor boards—scratched
I listen
Ear pressed to the surface
Masking woes
Stuck like a child's tongue
To an iced sign post

She sniffs
Coughs
Vomits—chunks

She calls for me—gurgles
Baby
Hold my hair out of my face
I can't breathe

No
Not natural.

She bleeds
Between her thighs
It runs pink on the tiles

Relief shuts the curtains
Inhales years of pain like exhaled smoke
We find comfort
In each others' ache
Palms sticky—with excreted insanity
Accentuating these faulty lifelines

I'm done, she says.
This is enough.
I nod and wipe our blood between her eyes.

the encasing

This feverish cold sweat
is not my body fighting
a disease—it's mother's
cold breath on my warm
glass shield; attempting
to stab its leather casing.

not better late than never

You decide
to bake cookies—the kind
that Mummies make
for working bees.
But have you noticed,
I'm eighteen?

Look—add some hash
and it's a done deal.
Hmm?
I shouldn't be taking drugs?
Well.
Huh.
Funny that.

You should
have considered
this aversion
before pumping
your own
veins full
of crap.

Who's the black
kettle now, huh?
And isn't it a bit late?
Where were the cookies

on the day
I came home
from my first
day of school
and found you
unconscious

on the kitchen floor?

I could have eaten those
instead of nails and hair.

part III

the lost song

Poised
Slender arch in silhouette
Laced with enigma
Fevered freedom—
Fervour for the last tune
Hot breath bedews notes with ink tails
Swans on printed streams—seams on sand dunes
Hands rise—wings with needs
Hover—hang—
Non compos mentis rail
Wan fingers search the keys like brail

there is no emptiness

Emptiness is not
the flush of flat
chords in your sigh.

Nor is it the tenor
ache; the hum of hope
resisting suicide.

Or fertile pain
becoming serum in
an ominous syringe.

Emptiness is fullness,
annulled by
noxious pills.

it's days like this...
i wish...

Your rages are like a storm;
there is always an eye
of calm
when you sit
and smoke
and watch
the leaves
blow in
the wind
in our front yard.

I take advantage of days like this—
the short moments when you sit
in your wicker chair—
garnished with red
and white polka dot cushions
stained yellow from your teas.

I crouch down beside by you.
Toxic scent in skin.
Warmth radiates like steam from a kettle;
I wish
I could catch
your mist in a jar
and release it,
for comfort,

when I can't sleep.
You smile at oblivion—
a cloud of smoke-filled code.
What are you thinking?
How you might craft your grand exit?
How much debris should you leave this time?
I don't care.

I just want to sit with you—
smiling at nothingness
with you.
Pretending the mist won't ever fade.

I stroke your hand
that grips the arm of the wicker chair.
Crunch.
A splinter
drops to the floor.
It hits carpet—
debris;
a prelude to your finale.

freckles

sun tattoos your pain
through rain in your open pores
freckles of failed dreams

failure...

breaks pale dreamers;
charm demotes passionate
slaps—fence-sitting
idle-izes silver spoons.
Crotchéd eyelashes
leak—gush—fail,
dreamer's pail breaks.

We're here to drown.

rat snake

she's a snake
taking short cuts

instead of shedding skin,
she puts layers *on*,
until she becomes protuberant — fetid
and is forced to discard
ten layers at once
too fast;

you only have to look away
for
one
second
when

a porous lump
of urbanized intentions
overpowering and grotesque
medusa's head lie
in front of you
on the table
a tentacle paroxysm
too big to disregard,
too big to accept like a piece of gum
rooted

she's putrid redundant agendas
that creep up on you like bathroom grime—
one day they're non-existent
the next your ceiling is infested
a basement brimmed with rats

reptiles, rodents—her mind, body, soul

crooked

Truncated intentions
float inside crooked halos;
pierced love, anti-hearts;
no reds, no arrows.
Practiced domestics,
thoughtful efforts,
lullaby's linked goodbyes
nothing buys
unconditional affection;
not money, not sweets,
not kisses, not time …
or maybe time reversed;
a chance to swim
with toddler limbs.

motion sickness

metallic tastes smear
strict tongue with backseat drive
shift of malady

fork

Four holes scar your tongue,
but they're not the only
holes in you.
Perhaps that's why

you eat with your hands;
weary of men
with cutlery.
Perhaps that's why

between your lips
I always have to ask
you to repeat yourself.
Perhaps that's why

when you're not guarding
your mouth, you like to scream;
to scare off other forks.
Perhaps that's why

I still love you.
Because you're damaged like me.

the seraph

I strain to suck her air below the surface of the stream. The swell is not sufficient, but it keeps my senses alive. Just enough for secrets to seep in. But I'd prefer solitude, you know. To taste saccharine on my lips. The torment she can keep. Otherwise there's no room to spread my six wings, in this pool of slime water, created for her satisfaction. I can't even cleanse them—these wings. These limbs she supposes she's blessed me with. The stream is too shallow; my lungs full of emptiness. *It's for Us*, she said, when she swallowed my life—my childhood. *I'm dying*, she whispered, sombreness sparkling in her eyes. It's not why I summoned her, to make me mourning sick. I wanted someone to save me from swallowing her stream; from her slimy water infecting my veins. Then I saw her rise, secure in her saintly skin. Free. When I rose to the surface; when I yelped at the sight of my oily feathers.

withered with age

Time has rendered
your songs naked
aged breasts.

What were martyrs
of feminist liberation,
aspiration,
makers of ministry,
are now flat,
volume-less,
sacks of dry juice,
wrinkled by addiction;
polluted with poison.

Phoney attempts
to revive them
with tactile props
is not going to deem
talent revitalized.

All you have left
is sagging skin
underneath
flashy covers.
And it's your fault.

If you had listened,
your songs would
still be
bouncing
with life.
And so would you.

seeking refuge

She places her hand on my body.
it's wet; hot—initiating mould.
I can feel each cell as it divides
and multiplies. She burrows
through pores fraught to reach
the river of austerity, flowing
through pipes of acerbic blood—
like dying sperm, mistaking liberty
for asylum, in search of a membrane
to weep in. She removes her hand
from my body. I grab her earth;
skin melting between my fingers; pulses.
I reapply her, as if ice to a bruise.

life in a box

At first light, I awake, without the son of dawn, climbing through my window like God's been born. I hear cats' cries echo through still-dark streets. They disturb the false peace, where the hungry die. Glass breaks, screams are heard. An illusion of Jesus and his holy word. Calls of fear fall from damp brick walls. Damp brick walls fall from fearful calls. Houses crumble. The men folk skint. The rich keep buying fur coats made of mink. But I do not wish to trade night for day. How would I sleep without the silver moon, making shadows of leaves, on the walls, in my room? So, please save those words of guilt—those words you use to persuade the world you're an angel deep down. Stop preaching little nothings about healing, curing, becoming holy, in my deaf ear. Though I may be hoping and praying, every year, I do not wish to call upon you. I treasure this life of solitude. In this box. Without fear. Without reason. Without you.

twisted velvet chains

You
told me
I was ugly.

You told
me
I was cold.

You said
my surface beauty
meant compassionless.

You
called me
selfish bitch.

You called
me
trashy slut.

You stuck your fingers
in your cunt,
ran them through my tangled hair,
spat in my face —
I let you.

You liked to
slap me.

You needed to
choke me.

You encouraged me
to drive a knife

into my trusting arm.

But still I stroked your cheek
when you'd overdose,
because I loved you
like a child
who had nowhere else to turn.

But, Mother
can you please
release me
from your twisted grip?
I know
it's not a prison cell,
but heavy grief grows mould.

I need to
clean these chains—
these strings of
velvet woe,
before these memories
stimulate one more
masticating echo.

the gutenberg bible

Her face, weary, depressed, on the brink of giving up. The left side dimly lit, the right side pitch black. Interdependence of opposites: yin and yang. Contaminating each other to form a temporary misconstruction of character; confused and simmered down to a childlike perception of right and wrong. Fragile Mum— as fragile as an infertile phoenix; as rare as the Gutenberg Bible, hieroglyphed black and white.

JUMP

hopes—pinned   down
town   bridge—broken
ridge—slippery cobbled
surface—magnet   static
waves—lift   like   hair
thin   volume—quiet
when   drowning—river
bed—swift   current
grave—muddy   death

below the rind

The clock ticks like a sewing needle tapping eggshell. In darkness, she walks toward the kitchen window. Moonbeams pass over her face like headlights through blinds. She leans her bony hip against the sink, squinting between shadows of the shrivelling citrus tree in her backyard. White light glimmers through her eyelashes. Tears are caught in them like drops of water in a web, creating prisms that resemble flecks of silver glitter. Over-ripe oranges perish on the concrete; the acidic scent of trodden rind wheedles its way through the cracked wooden frame of the window. It hisses like escaping gas. She thinks about herself rotting; staining every footpath she is bound to tread with her bitter memory; contaminating tongues with a tart taste at the mere mentioning of her name. But she wants to taste the *sweet* fruit—a need that has been harassing her ever since she died. She needs to know the real her; to learn to love 'the who' below her wilting, fetid dimpled skin.

snob

Sewer sides repulse
women like me who prefer
scent candles to death

science

thin trenches weave into skin
the treasures of age
blending physics with spirit
now you are in me

part IV

mama's gonna buy me a mocking bird

incision. bradawl. drain,
this liquid brain—bane
of smart pain—filtered.

long live the rock queen
of spades: in dirt, grime,
nursery rhyme; you say
loving that sweater, girl.

resurrected, below earth
is the woman who sings
for diamond rings, babe.

ashes

Green splashes sting my face with lament, as my oars push away a river of you, thick with disgust. Toffee in teeth. You hang on until I pry you off, push you down, wet wood, my will for you drown. Help me find the locket you once lost. I know it means more than I will, ever. If we were on land, I'd scorch you, rip you, burn you in a fire. But we are floating now. Aren't we? So I will soak you, drench you, make you soft and pliable. I'll squash you; roll you into a weeping porcelain ball. In the river. Secure waters, where I will never return.

the dolour thief

I turn off the ignition. For a split second, I wish I had a garage to gas myself in. I rest my arms, my head on the steering wheel. When did I realise, life does not heal? I *need* to cry, to feel, the emptiness, the ache. Not an ache. Hatred. A ghost. Breathing all my air. I look through the windshield at the trees struggling to shift in the thin hot breeze. I lean back in my seat and close my eyes— listen to the hum of sin brush against my skin. The only lingering proof left of you. Of *us*. I wish for sorrow to get caught on me like a broken nail in wool. To remind myself I'm human, that I can feel *pain*, that for once in *this* life I am allowed to, without constraint. It's time to bond with it, this grief. No pain? No relief. No relief? No joy. I must deem it vital to survival, change colour with its leaves. I'll become the leader of The Dolour Thieves.

killing me slowly

Remembering you
kills brain cells—
dozens from each emotion:
Anger, Grief, Acceptance.
Though on different days
AGA is GAA or
GAA is AAG—Argh!
Soon AGA will become
indifference. I'll wring you
out—wash your juice
down the drain. And
stop caring. But I want
to care. So could you
please stop killing brain
cells? Or I might have
to become an alcoholic.

organ charms

Grinding jaw against splintered bench, clear smears: ethical sheen. Umbilical chords imitate charm, hidden between enamelled prayer; left to mix into bites on my back. I squeeze scent from split ends, recalling your black frock brush over cheek; electric holy water seeping from my mouth, or was it yours, Mama.

disaster...

swirls, lost in a haze
since you left this crooked earth
feet never touch ground

in the back of his book

I go to bed early
to be away from you
though I do not want it
permanently, I do
want you
in my thoughts
where I want to write
think
in the orange bedside light
that makes my imagination glow
somehow I suck
up warmth
in two thick quilts
rain pounding on the tents
heater humming on full
the level you used to nag me about
while I read Raymond Carver
and wish to write something raw
I pick up my pencil
scribble this down
in the back of his book
I wonder if you would hear me
if I slipped my hand down my pants
I'd feel guilty
I haven't made love with him in five months

how did that happen?
I love him, but I need to be away from him too
with you still here
this makes no sense
written purposely —illegibly
so it can make sense to only me
I'll leave this open by my bed
perhaps he'll see it
and somehow understand

surfacescape

Black blocked
fringe like
guitar frets,
math genius
with specs,
only lesbians
ask for
autographs,
in the streets,
lanes, at
Paper Trains;
folded now,
famous four,
franchised
into
bipolar moods,
as staged as
selective hearing.
If bodies
could travel
like voices,
you could
be anywhere,
separating
in mist

like a ghost;
gothic rock
in black sheets
littered streets
your home.
In each and every
cityscape
you haunt
me with

your fringe,
your image,
your death.

solar emotion

A terrace of solar-panelled regrets
sucks in rays of gratitude
moments before I deactivate the grid.

the real you

I like to think I hated you because I didn't understand. But it's not, *really* the reason. It's because I put up a wall; didn't let you in—afraid you would corrupt me—declare your disorder permanent. But why? There were moments of lucidity—and I could see the difference between *you* and *it*. But while ignoring *it*, I ignored *you* too. I know that now. I know I ignored the two *you*s because I was afraid to lose the *real* you—afraid she might decide to never show her face again. I was afraid to love, too—because I had to love you both—be vulnerable—ready to jump—throw up the shield when the *you* I wanted to love hid behind your violent *it*. I'm sorry I didn't let my wall down. But I'm letting it down now. Is it too late? I know you might have been a wonderful mother, had the real *you* been allowed to play outside a little more often, without *it*.

perhaps if I

Do you think
we'd have been
friends in old age?
In the way you
used to hint at
in the mornings
with *that* smile
I refused to see?

Your voice would muffle
behind the crunch
of cornflakes—the swish
of milk between my teeth.
When I'd swallow,
you'd be looking at me
—head tilted—*that* smile
on the brink
of dwindling—corner twitch.

Oh, how I wish
I wasn't such
a cold-hearted teen
and listened
in those moments
when your voice

was gentle and warm;
when you needed
to love me;
when you needed
me to love you
despite the shit
you put me through.

Why didn't I see it then?
Why didn't I
stop chewing when
I saw *that* smile?

I wonder now
if I had hugged you,
given you what
you seemed to be
inadvertently asking for,
whether we'd be
friends today.

Perhaps if I'd hugged you
—said, *I love you*—
you wouldn't have killed yourself.

thorns like dough

Frail and thin, already in a coffin
on my couch, I slouch to melodies.
You remind me of poise;
I paint your eyebrows black—
the way they used to be.
You smile at someone who is not there;
absent, forgotten, all except your songs—
lyrics—dark, gothic rock on wilted petals;
stalks like roses, thorns like dough—now.
Will I ever listen again?
—the scch and crackle of your old records.
I want to remember,
when your music makes fresh tears.
And I cry, not from your music,
I cry because it might be where you left your soul.
All my life, I've been angry at skin and bone.
But forgot to listen. I will listen now.
the way life should have been—
I will remember you on vinyl.

acknowledgements

Many thanks to the editors of the following journals and anthologies where many of these poems have appeared, some in altered states: *Something From The Attic* (Static Movement); *Literary Foray* (Static Movement); *Static Poetry* (Static Movement); *Static Poetry II* (Static Movement); *Dark Poetry* (Static Movement); *Ramshackle Review*; *The Stray Branch*; *Cordite Poetry Review*; *The Lascaux Review*; *Visceral Uterus*; *Red River Review*.

A special thanks to my parents—Erika Bach and Demetri Vlass, Spilios—my one and only for life, Nicole, Dawn, Janice, Alaine, Angie, Glynis, and Angela for their support, help, friendship and encouragement toward the making of this book.

And of course, a very special thanks to Amie McCracken for her enormous help in producing *The Bell Collection* edition.

Enjoyed this book?
Go to *vineleavespress.com/books*
to find more from *The Bell Collection.*

To sign up to Jessica's newsletter
and/or connect with her on social media
go to *jessicabellauthor.com/contact*.

Are you a writer?
You might be interested in Jessica's
Writing in a Nutshell series.

www.ingramcontent.com/pod-product-compliance
Lightning Source LLC
Chambersburg PA
CBHW051733040426
42447CB00008B/1106